*The Aquinas Lecture, 1972*

# PSYCHE AND CEREBRUM

Under the auspices of the
Wisconsin-Alpha Chapter of Phi Sigma Tau

By

JOHN N. FINDLAY, M.A. Oxon., Ph.D.

MARQUETTE UNIVERSITY PRESS
MILWAUKEE
1972

Library of Congress Catalog Card Number: 72-76593

ISBN 0-87462-137-2

PRINTED
IN U·S·A·

# Prefatory

The Wisconsin-Alpha-Chapter of Phi Sigma Tau, the National Honor Society for Philosophy at Marquette University, each year invites a scholar to deliver a lecture in honor of St. Thomas Aquinas, whose feastday was formerly March 7. The lectures are customarily given on the first Sunday of March. The 1972 Aquinas Lecture *Psyche and Cerebrum* was delivered on March 5 in Todd Wehr Chemistry by Professor John N. Findlay, Clark Professor of Moral Philosophy and Metaphysics, Yale University.

Professor John Niemeyer Findlay was born in Pretoria, Transvaal, South Africa on November 25, 1903. He earned his A.B. in 1923 and his M.A. in 1924 at the University of Pretoria. He was a Rhodes Scholar for three years at Balliol College, Oxford, where he earned the A.B. and in 1930 the M.A. He earned his Ph.D. at the University of Gratz in 1934.

Professor Findlay began his teaching career at Otago, Dunedin, New Zealand.

During the school year of 1938–1939 he studied under Rudolf Carnap, Martin Heidegger and G. E. Moore. In 1954 he was Professor of Philosophy at Grahamstown, S.A., then for two years at Natal, S.A. In 1948 he came to England, teaching at King's College, Newcastle-upon-Tyne from 1948 to 1951, and at King's College, University of London, from 1951 to 1966. He was President of the Aristotelian Society in 1955 and the next year was elected Fellow in the British Academy. He gave the Gifford Lectures in 1964 and again in 1965. Prof. Findlay moved to the United States in 1966, teaching one year at the University of Texas and then, since 1967, at Yale University.

Professor Findlay's thought can be designated in three periods. First, his interest was in idealistic and speculative philosophy, especially that of Bergson, Spinoza, Hegel, Plato and Plotinus. The middle period was devoted to the realism and analysis of Russell, Moore, Meinong, Carnap and the later Wittgenstein. The third period, from 1957 on, represents a return,

with considerable critical and methodo-
logical improvements, to his original philosophical interests.

The numerous publications of Professor Findlay include: *Meinong's Theory of
Objects,* Oxford: Oxford University Press,
1933; *Hegel: A Re-Examination,* London:
Allen and Unwin, 1958; *Language, Mind
and Value,* London: Allen and Unwin,
1963; *The Discipline of the Cave,* London: Allen and Unwin, 1966; *The Transcendence of the Cave,* London: Allen and
Unwin, 1967; *Axiological Ethics,* London:
Macmillan, 1970; some thirty articles in
three languages in philosophical journals.
To these publications Phi Sigma Tau is
pleased to add: *Psyche and Cerebrum.*

# Psyche and Cerebrum

The present lecture deals with the relations of three dimensions of our intelligent, conscious being-in-the world which I shall distinguish as the behavioural, the phenomenological and the connective or neural. Our being consciously alive *in* the world and *to* the world involves all these dimensions. We must be acted upon by the world and be reactive to it like any other worldly object, but to be *consciously* alive, we must have a world which is there *for* us, given *to* us in a vast variety of manners, lights and guises, and we must in addition have a nervous system and brain, and above all a brain-bark or cortex, in order to be effectively in the world and in order for the world to be effectively there for us. But how the members of this ill-assorted triumvirate contribute severally to our conscious, living being-in-the-world is a profoundly obscure and controversial matter: it has been so since the very beginning

of modern philosophy, and has remained
so despite the shifts of emphasis due to
the ever changing discoveries of science.
These discoveries have seemed again and
again to revolutionize the total scene, and
to inundate all its well-known landmarks,
but again and again, with the retreat of
the flood, the old landmarks have reas-
serted themselves, perhaps a bit covered
over with sand and silt, but preserving the
same general configuration. The surmise
indeed suggests itself to the critical philosopher that here we are up against a dis-
tinction of categories, of things that cannot
be established or overturned by experiment, because they are the presuppositions
of experiment, because they must, in general terms, be as they are if we are to be
able to observe anything empirically or to
learn from our observations. Possibly the
general nature of these factors, and the
general character of their interrelations,
are all necessary and categorial: they
provide a framework within which science
can do its detailed investigative work and
achieve its peculiar discoveries, but they

are not anything on which science, rather than profound philosophical reflection, can hope to throw final light.

There is, however, also the interesting possibility, which will be touched on at the end of this lecture, that there is something very special, and at once advantageous and disadvantageous, about the particular way of being consciously alive in the world that involves so special a mediating embodiment as the cerebrum or its outer bark or cortex. The human cerebrum and its cortex are plainly, on the one hand, the highest product of organic evolution, and represent the highest pinnacle of complex integration and flexibility of response that organic evolution has achieved; on the other hand it is highly arguable that there is something cut-off, divorced from the grass-roots of being, something stilted, parasitic and falsely privileged about this cortical, cerebral life of ours, and that our philosophical difficulties are among the many fruits of this falsely stilted position. Like St. Simeon Stylites on his column we are so elevated above the rough-and-tumble of the market-place that we are fundamentally confused as to what may be going on there. And scientists, I would suggest, are as much or more in the position of St. Simeon Stylites than ordinary people. Possibly if one goes down the evolutionary ladder, or simply goes down to the humble units in one's own body, one has in one's hands cases of life and experience that are much less cut off from environing reality and from other conscious existences, and so much less angled and paradoxical and prone to philosophical difficulties than our own conscious existence necessarily is. Postibly also there are levels of conscious being to which we can in some illuminated moments attain, and which we may enjoy more fully in some after-condition, where the defects of cerebral mediation and instrumentation will be set aside, with a consequent reduction in the philosophical and other riddles which beset us in our present life. These suggestions will recur at the end of this lecture, though we shall make them without confidence. Of all riddles in the world those which attend on our involvement with brains are among the most intractable.

I must, however, leave generalities and proceed to say something about the three dimensions of our conscious being-in-the-world that I have distinguished. The first, the behavioural, is one whose logic has only been worked out in the present century, from Watson through Tolman, Holt, Dewey and Mead to Ryle; though at first seemingly tractable and straightforward, it has proved as rich in mare's-nests and metaphysics as any other conceptual dimension. Only to a few men of faith like Professor Skinner of Harvard does it still seem simple and clear. Quite plainly, as we are living beings consciously in the world, the world and its contents and remote structural appendages has had to impinge upon us causally in countless direct and indirect ways, either through the senses or through revivals of past sensuous encounters, or through countless subtle internal transformations, or through countless social linguistic influences impinging on us from the environment, and we have had to respond to all these influences stemming from the world in a variety of direct and simple, or widely modified and unsimple ways. At first the notion of a behavioural response seems straightforward and unambiguous: we can *see* or *hear* a man striking the table, raising his voice, swivelling his eyeballs to left and right, and so on. It is, however, plain that a behavioural response is only a behavioural response if it is a response *to* something or other, and what one is responding to, even if one is an animal, is not at all obvious from the situation open to examination. The behaving being may not be responding to anything actually present in the situation, but to something present in similar situations in the past, or to something quite hidden or connected with the present situation only by a long track or route. It may even be something wholly general such as food or a mate, or something wholly non-existent and imaginary. A savage responds to mysterious effluences like *mana*, or mysterious performances like casting the evil eye or trapping a man's soul through his photograph, and so on. And even if there is a response to something plainly present in the environment, it is not clear from what is done in what light the object or situation is being responded to, whether as triangular, or dangerous, or as a sign of the wanted road, etc., etc. What the environmental situation is for anyone only comes out after an exhaustive testing of responses in several situations. And not only is it not clear what we are responding to, and how it comes before us, but also what sort of a response we are making to it. In eating a white powder, are we attempting suicide, or eating what we take to be a sweetmeat, or pretending to do one or the other, or is it merely a link in a complex purposive chain, etc., etc? All these are points which require indefinite testing to establish what they portend. The exigencies of the context, or the devised simplicities of the laboratory situation, may render this unnecessary, but this can only be so because so much general testing has been done in the past.

What a being is doing can then only
be understood in the total constellation of
its contemporary and past responses and
those of the beings which influence it and
among which it lives. And our contempla-
tion must extend beyond the actual into
the hypothetical or the probable. All this
means that the behavioural dimension
of our conscious being-in-the-world is a
vastly metaphysical affair, not all lying on
the surface as the early behaviourists, tired
of mentalistic mystifications, supposed and
hoped. It manifests what we may call
remote intentionality or transcendent concern, and it may be concerned with what
is distant or vaguely general or even unreal
as much as with what is concrete and
immediate; it is also invariably 'angled,'
concerned with what it is concerned with
from a subtle, not easily ascertainable
point of view. It also has a higher-order
universality both in what it responds to,
and in the nature of its response, which
enables it to substitute one line of action
for another and one object of reaction for
another almost without limit. It has, fur-

ther, a strange overall unity which makes it hard and complex to study, and it has a power of modifying its responses and retreating to higher levels of universality, and new specifications of the same, which is neither routine nor random, but in the best sense of the word insightful and creative. Behaviour thus qualified can be interpreted, and interpreted with confidence in very many cases, but its interpretation involves a taking seriously of much that is neither concrete nor real, and vastly much that is dispositional rather than actual. Behaviour is an essential dimension of conscious-being-in-the-world, not some irrelevant, outward 'expression' of it as earlier philosophers supposed; it is not, however, a dimension that lends itself to mere observation or that is free from profound philosophical obscurities. Its obscurity does not, of course, diminish it; it renders it non-trivial and worthy of philosophical consideration.

It is, however, impossible to stop at this point in mind-theory, nor is what one has capable of standing on its own legs if not

supplemented by quite another, phenomenological approach. The world must not
only be there with the living conscious
being responding to it; the world and all
its contents and attachments must also be
there *for* the intelligent, conscious being
or must be capable of being there *for* it,
and being there for it, or present to it,
is not, despite many attempts in that
direction, analysable in terms of mere
behaviour, however well adapted to the
situation. There must, in order that there
should be conscious being-in-the-world,
be something that I shall speak of meta-
phorically, in full awareness of its dualistic
dangers, as a 'phenomenological screen' on
which objects including the viewing subject must appear before the viewing subject, must be given or intended in a variety
of different ways. It is plain that in default
of such a phenomenological dimension or
its possibility, the behavioural dimension
would not be one of conscious life at all;
it would not even, particularly in respect
of its objects, be capable of a satisfac-
tory conceptual pinning-down. It is only

because we know what it is like to have some object before one, or consciously given to one, that one can endow behaviour with a direction that, as behaviour actually comes before us, is not obvious at all. And it is more than arguable that the whole world and its contents and attachments would be nothing that we could talk about or refer to understandingly unless this second phenomenological dimension were *also* capable of being talked about and understood. For it is only possible to talk about or recognize this or that thing or state of affairs in the world, if it is also possible to talk about and recognize the acts of reference and understanding in which that thing or state of affairs is referred to or understood. To understand objects and states of affairs is to understand the understanding of them, and a world whose understanding we did not understand would be an unworld, a mere nothing, not an object of significant reference. Mental events are not, as some have imagined, a queer set of substitute acts that we *sometimes* do 'in our heads,' and that then do duty for other public acts that have nothing private about them. There is no public act that has not its private, phenomenological, subjective side, for whether we write on paper or utter words in a public debate or physically fight with someone, we do so *for ourselves* as well as for others or as a mere fact in the world; we are conscious of how we move our fingers, shape our lips or seize someone by the forelock, and the same deeds which in one context are part of the public world are also, in another context, tinged with all the hues of subjectivity which none but ourselves can quite fully understand. The same act that from one point of view is a public phenomenon is from another point of view a private, personal phenomenon: we experience the two-sidedness in our own case, and we know that it is present in the case of others.

The logic of conscious grasp, of intentional presence, is, however, far from obvious and easy, and it has only been (more or less) satisfactorily unravelled in the past century, beginning with Brentano's masterly *Psychology from the Empirical Standpoint* in 1874, and carried further, though with disturbing irrelevances, by such intentionalist and phenomenological thinkers as Alexius Meinong, Edmund Husserl, Roman Ingarden, Moritz Geiger, Maurice Merleau-Ponty, as well as by some wilder, but at times happily inspired, existentialists such as Heidegger and Sartre. Though they have many divergences of doctrine and terminology, all may be said to believe in a sort of immanent transcendence, a capacity to point consciously to something beyond oneself and to make it the target of one's concern, without thereby affecting it causally, or being affected by it causally, or in fact going beyond the circle of one's personal life at all. This property of remote concern has the further remarkable feature that it may terminate on things unreal and not there at all, or there only *for* the concerned subject, but that it may also terminate on things real and independent of the subject, though also there for it, and that are at times known by the subject to be thus independent of the subject, so that there is a perfect and known coincidence (not a dubious correspondence) of things as they are in themselves with things as they appear to rationally certificated, 'evident' thought. It also has the remarkable property of being always in some manner and degree present to itself, so that in being aware of this or that transcendent thing or state of affairs, we also *ipso facto* live through our own awareness of this or that thing or state of affairs, and can, if we will, bring this self-experience into a more developed, self-focused, analytic form.

The realm of mental references proliferates into infinite variety: one can be conscious of things clearly or marginally, predicatively or non-predicatively, sensuously or imaginally or symbolically or merely notionally, believingly or doubtingly or entertainingly, approvingly or disapprovingly, hopefully or fearfully and so on. The study of all these attitudes and their relationships to one another and to their objects is a matter of infinite complication, in whose unravelling an analyst like Husserl is supremely skilled. The phenomenological dimension repeats the properties of the behavioural dimension: remote concern, high-level universality and substitutability, angled presentation of objects in definite lights, and the abstracted giving of specific angles as such, profound flexibility and open universality of appearance and connections, so that new angles of vision are constantly emerging and guiding the appearances into novel channels in a way that is neither routine nor random. But there is much less metaphorical obscurity in the phenomenological than in the behavioural sector: we do not need to test ourselves in a variety of real and actual situations, in order to know that we are afraid, for example, that we may have said the wrong thing and committed a social blunder, and that we must now have recourse to some desperate manoeuvre to cover up our embarrassment. All this is clear to us who are embarrassed, and it is clear to others to whom we *tell* of our embarrassment. But though less obscure than the behavioural dimension, it is from another point of view much more parasitic and dependent: the world appears to us only in broken snatches which are never fully executed or fitted together, the point of view is continuously being shifted, the whole proceeding is constantly being interrupted by periods of unconsciousness or sleep. Those idealist philosophers who believe the phenomenological perspective to be also the only real one, have to put up with a reality that is largely made up of fragments and hopes, or to supplement these by the activities of an unconscious mind or a God. We can at best say that our moments of lucid grasp are always hedged around with an infinite number of *readinesses* for lucid consciousness, which hover about on the perimeter of conscious experience, and which, though not brought to fulfilment, yet remain real forces in the phenomenological and the behavioural field, and channel the appearances and our reactions to them, even though they do not offer themselves to our conscious self-scrutiny. I have, to use Husserl's expression, always something *im*

*Griff*, on hand, in grasp, ready to transform itself into full conscious grasp should occasion offer, but still relevantly influential even if not allowed or able to develop. This dispositional surrounding of the phenomenological dimension is as all-pervasive as is that of the behavioural dimension; both are therefore in much the same manner metaphysical, supplementing the given with entities that are certainly real and felt 'with our bones' even if not, in some transparent manner, given.

We have therefore our two dimensions of our conscious life-in-the-world: the external, causal, behavioural dimension and the internal, phenomenological, intentional dimension. Mediating the two, and perhaps exhibiting both causal and intentional features, is the intercalated dimension of the neurones and the neural structures, and, at the highest level, of the cortex. It is plain that phenomenology and high-grade action are not mediated by the body as a whole. Despite the phenomenological showings, the psyche would not appear to exist *tota in toto* and *tota in*

*qualibet parte* as Thomas and others supposed, but to have a *direct* relation only
to certain higher regions of the nervous
system and in particular to those of the
cortex or outer bark of the cerebrum.
Plainly we have no clairvoyant perception
of the things around us, or if we have it is
grossly overlaid; the world is there for us
by stimulating sense-terminals which agi-
tate nerves which cause disturbances in
appropriate cortical regions. The older
philosophers conceived of appearances
called 'sensations' entering on the phenomenological stage, and there undergo-
ing an elaborate process of interpretative
recostuming and lighting till they become
the perceived objects that we now recognize. We now know that the elaborate
process of recostuming takes place at
lower levels and is not based on the redun-
dant sensations that are artificially ana-
lysed out of perceptual experience. Sometimes such sensations are wholly absent:
it is quite outside of the phenomenological
sphere that disparate visual stimulations
give rise to percepts of depth, or aural

stimulations to percepts of the direction
of sound, or stimulations of the semi-circu-
lar canals to percepts of posture and direction. In some cases there *have* been phases
of conscious interpretation which have in
course of time lapsed into unawareness,
but in many cases the 'interpretation' has
been pre-conscious, and in some sense sub-
cortical or pre-cortical. Our position in fact
is like that of some high-born aristocrat
who receives all his food beautifully
cooked and prepared by unknown minions
in the kitchen, and who also (as happens in
Japanese inns) has a beautiful lady to put
the food in his mouth. And on the other
side all our elaborately adjusted intelligent
responses can be shown to involve an elaborate series of nerve-pullings which influence vastly many relaxing and contracting
muscles, and receive a regulated feed-back
from those muscles which promotes further
exercises in wire-pulling. We are all, it
would appear, marionettes, members of
the family of Pinocchio; our simplest acts
at any moment involve a continuum of
back-feeding wire-pulls. To imagine what

is cerebrally happening when a lovely girl
in lightsome mood runs along the seashore
playing with a barking dog is to carry the
complications of puppetry to a point where
they become unpleasant: surely so many
mechanisms cannot be needed to effect a
result as unitary and as gaily simple! But
plainly conscious being-in-the-world is an
affair of great complexity and difficulty: it
involves the imposition of a new kind of
integration and a governance by general
patterns and remote intentional objects on
a rabble of molecules that are not readily
integrated into higher unities of any sort,
which do not readily follow patterns which
are not those of their isolated selves, and
whose commerce with intentional objects,
if they have any, is certainly of the vaguest
and the slightest. So that only by organiz-
ing and regimenting them in that quite
extraordinary way in which they are orga-
nized and regimented in the cerebrum and
nervous system can we achieve that ordered perception of the environment and
that adjusted response to its details which
conscious being-in-the-world involves.

But our subservience to our cellular and molecular henchmen and the mechanical chains in which they are ordered arguably goes much further. They not only present us with doctored and slanted pictures of the environment, and not only carry out our executive decisions, but, like an intrusive bureaucracy, take part in all the proceedings of the council chamber and throughout channel its deliberations and decisions. It is not enough that we should have been through certain experiences in the past; our access to them plausibly demands a touching-off by the henchmen who have also, in a humbler capacity, been through them. Without their cooperation a mere recall or an imaginatively modified replay would not for some strange reason be possible. And it seems likely that even our most attenuated, higher-order understandings and decisions, which involve a readiness to encounter or imagine countless sorts of things or to make countless verbal or wordless references to them or to do countless things that would count as responses to them, involve some sort of

complex, silent play on the cerebral organ,
a pulling out of certain stops and a putting
of a damper on others, even if no actual
sound emerges from our metaphorical
instrument. It seems further plausible to
hold that some of the high-grade unconscious rearrangements of our total readinesses, from which full-fledged conscious
phenomena and well-adjusted actions alike
issue, is a rearrangement in which the
cerebral henchmen or organ-stops or however they may be described play a significant part. When we display that inspired
absence of mind which is so misleadingly
called 'wit' or 'presence of mind,' it seems
arguable that they motivate a doing or a
saying of the 'right thing' long before its
content or its rightness have been pro-
jected on to the phenomenological screen.
All these facts, and likely extensions of
facts, prompt an inclination to pass from
a view in which we, as conscious living
beings involved in the world, are also
involved in such unconscious use of the
cerebrum as of some instrument through
which we play upon the world and the

world plays upon us, to a view in which
the cerebrum rather does everything and
is responsible for everything, and in which
the phenomenological total picture before
us and the ordered behaviour that we exe-
cute are alike cerebral manifestations. It
is then possible to drift to a view in which
the phenomenological subject becomes a
sort of happy *fainéant*, contemplating and
enjoying processes which he neither ini-
tiates nor controls, like a child watching
television in a modern household; but this
picture soon shifts, by an inherent dialectic, to a view in which we *identify* ourselves with the cerebrum, which is alike
responsible for all the appearances before
us and for all our conscious reactions. The
cerebrum then becomes the true man, the
homunculus concealed in the ivory tower
of the skullbones, to whom we must attrib-
bute all our highest perceptive, cogitative,
emotional and practical feats. It ceases to
be a mere corpus of convoluted grey cells
framing a core of white connective fibres,
and becomes a metaphysically active reality, referring, generalizing, integrating and

innovating in a manner never routine nor random: as Hegel said of the skull-bones of the phrenologists, in reducing spirit to the action of these cells we endow these cells with all the properties of spirit.

I believe, however, that this dialectic has carried us too far, and that we have abused our undoubted privilege of saying what we like provided we understand and keep to the rules which are laid down for such saying. We cannot, with due respect to the affinities of things, quite push the cerebral contribution to this limit: it can at best be regarded as instrumental extension of a life which uses it, not as giving that life itself nor as an extension of it. The difficulties in the way of a thoroughgoing cerebralism are logical: they rest on the difficulty of modelling something that displays remote intentionality in a medium that only displays fully actual, descriptive structures, and in modelling high-level universality, and, more importantly, the everlasting, open retreat to ever higher levels of universality, in a medium that cannot reflect all the higher-level affinities

and logical properties that are thus impli-
cated. As Wittgenstein said of the theory
of the perception of space as due to the
putting on of spatial spectacles, the explanation has not the logical multiplicity of
what it is devised to explain. It is no good
attributing everything to the cerebrum if
we are not prepared and also not able to
think of it as the sort of thing to which
such attributions can be significantly made,
and if we are not prepared or able to evolve
a view of it which engenders a true iso-
morphism between it and various behavioural and phenomenological features. Now
it is highly arguable that, when we consider remote intentionality, we have an
adjustment to what lies at the object-end
of our references rather than to what lies
at the personal, immediate end: it is what
we are dealing with, rather than our own
impression of it, that determines how our
perceptual and thought-extrapolations develop and how we react to their objects,
and it is hard to see how that which is not
mirrored even in the stimuli which affect
our bodies, and which may not even have

any reality, can be precisely mirrored in cerebral structures and changes which cannot readily be credited with a concern for objects and connections beyond themselves. A neurone could just thinkably, by a suitable anthropomorphism, be supposed to be socially embarrassed by the conduct of a neighbouring neurone which perhaps conducted impulses too readily or did so unsuitably, but can we meaningfully attribute to it concern, or anything isomorphic with a concern, that the total person feels in some socially embarrassing situation when he sees some other total person behaving unsuitably, and wonders how he can plausibly tone down his companion's social gaffe? Perhaps some have the wit to see how this is possible, but to me it sounds like showing how black marks on paper can, in default of suitable interpreters, touch off a revolution or an execution. It is easy to say how the stimuli which impress themselves on our sense-organs at a given time can be precisely mirrored in the pattern of certain brain-excitations or their reactivation; it is not so easy to see how the objective sense of these stimuli or excitations, changing from moment to moment, should be so mirrored. Despite the ingenuity of Koffka in his remarkable *Principles of Gestalt Psychology*, a masterpiece of speculative neurology, important in virtue of its very unsuccess, it is not very easy to see how the pattern of some joke should round itself off after the manner of a sensory pattern, and how it should be able to transfer its influence to a whole series of further jokes obeying the same principles. A half-sketched circle might plausibly be able to transform itself into a completed circle through the action of neural and ultimately of physico-chemical forces, but I cannot see that this is possible in the case of a joke or a series of jokes. Such perception and such a sense of humour I cannot, despite great good will, attribute to the cerebral henchmen, either alone or in any combination.

This leads us on to stress the high-level universality of the more inspired conscious performances: their guidance by, and their procedure along, constantly *profounder* relations of resemblance and affinity and logical connection and not by anything obviously there in the environmental or cerebral situation. We see an identity of principle in quite disparate phenomena as when Verlaine likened autumn to the long sob of a violin in tune with his own monotonous mood. It is also shown when we switch style or skill to a quite different pattern of action in a truly innovating, creative manner. What is remarkable about the phenomenological, behavioural subject is, moreover, the *open* nature of its sensitivity to universality in its free creativity: it makes and unmakes its programmes as it goes along and ascends to ever higher styles of coordination without ever being either wholly routine or wholly random in its performances. It may be true that there is no performance for which a good robot cannot be programmed, even to the writing of poems more or less like those of Verlaine, but there is a whole world of logical difference between saying that for every performance there is some robot that could be programmed to perform it, and saying

there is some robot which could be programmed to perform any and every performance. The order of the quantifiers
makes a notorious difference to the truth-
value, and yet this is a truism of the func-
tional calculus which many arguments
ignore. Yet the capacity of the behavioural
and phenomenological subject is precisely
to change its rules almost without limit and
yet not by chance: it sees or feels its way
into new, higher styles of universality. The
German idealists attributed properties
which they called 'infinity' and 'absolute
negativity' to the conscious person: such
a person could never be committed to anything wholly definite or finite, but could
always revise itself further. I do not know
how quite such boundless negativity can
be attributed to the cerebrum *qua* cerebrum, much as I am willing to allow it *some*
spontaneity of response: it can perhaps
innovate, even on its own, but can it innovate in the indefinite syntheses of high-
level meanings, which appear to have
nothing to do with what we take it to be?
Even if all past acts and encounters were

mirrored one for one in the cortex, and even if each distinguishable abstract feature had a separate 'centre' to deal with it, I still cannot see how *objectively* appropriate selections could be made from what is called the stored cortical 'information,' or how *objectively* suitable combinations of the abstracted features could be arrived at. Obviously the whole view of the cerebrum as the sole agent behind behaviour and phenomenology is wholly unacceptable. It involves, it is plain, an ignoring of distinct logical types, of categorial distinctions, and those who confuse types or categories we know never prosper.

Wittgenstein said that the meaning of words was not anything inwardly or outwardly correlated with them, but lay in their use, in what they led us to expect and do and in what circumstances. I am far from endorsing everything that Wittgenstein says, but on this occasion I shall borrow a leaf from his book. I shall say that the meaning of cerebral structure and processes is something which goes indefinitely beyond them and which can therefore be meaningfully equated with the manner in which they are used, both actively and interpretatively, by the living, conscious being-in-the-world. The cerebrum is not some perfect face by studying which in isolation we shall be able to see exactly the content and drift of every perception, thought, feeling, dream, wish or voluntary decision; it is a face as imperfectly expressive as our ordinary one, the sense of whose changes lies in the endlessly unfolding vistas of phenomenology and the endlessly unfolding feats of adjusted response. That the meaning of the cerebrum and its structures lies in its use, will not, however, necessarily drive us to believe in some quite immaterial user, only in a user who, though enmeshed in a cerebral organ in a manner far more intimate than Aristotle ever suspected, none the less, in certain features of what it does and understands, rises above what is merely attributable to its bodily organ, considered merely as the units of which it consists. We may in fact follow certain wise philosophers, including Hegel, in believing that unorganized mat-

ter must be credited with a steady move-
ment towards the integration, the intentionality, and the high-level universality
and innovative openness which are characteristic of our conscious life-in-the-world,
and which appears in those imperfectly developed but none the less effective readinesses for consciousness or likenesses of
consciousness which we find throughout
the nervous system.

I return briefly, at the end of my lecture, to the suggestion I made at the beginning that the puzzles that vex us in regard
to the cerebrum, as well as many of our
other philosophical problems, may themselves be the product of something peculiar
in our situation in which the cerebrum also
plays a part. The philosophy of mechanis-
tic neuralism, with its deep unsuccess and
its generation of philosophical surds, may
itself be a product of cerebral involvement:
it may in fact be the philosophy *of* the
cerebrum in more senses than one. Let me
suggest, without working my suggestions
out in detail, how cerebrally mediated conscious life may introduce surds into our

general view of the world. It may do so
precisely by depriving us of the undoc-
tored sensations which the older psycholo-
gists and philosophers believed in, and
which in some sense represent the joint
actuality of objects and ourselves, and giving us instead a world of remote objects,
all fully interpreted, which stand over
against our subjectivity without needing
to give us the sensations in which subject
and object meet, and in which both what
is in us and what transcends us are felt as
in unity and not separated by a gulf. This
gulf is particularly deep in the case of the
perception of others which now appears
something remote, inferential, requiring a
strange exercise of self-transcendence,
whereas in the case of simpler organisms,
hypothetically plants, there may be an os-
motic sharing of the experiences of others
which we in certain moods adumbrate but
never effectively arrive at. Our cerebrally
mediated perception is further such as to
dirempt the perceived world into neat
bright units set apart from each other, each
given by a separate informational channel

and so absolutely distinct. We accordingly
tend to think in terms of hard, bright, separate factors, capable of being put together
and taken apart without change, and to see
their intercourse as something rigorously
prefigured in each and admitting nothing
of the creative or the truly innovative. And
it is the remote, dirempted character of our
cerebral dealings that makes the cerebrum
itself seem such a dead, senseless thing, so
utterly unlike the behavioural and phenomenological developments that pass
through it and which then tempts us to
reduce the latter to the former, and so to
indulge in all the hopeless mystifications
of speculative neurology, whether mecha-
nistic or animistic. Speculative and even
experimental neurology is itself a product
of our cerebral involvement: it is the
strained reflection of what is arguably a
quite special condition. We may go further
and hold that a great deal of scientific
methodology, with its belief in invariant,
isolable factors and rigorous laws govern-
ing their interaction, is itself a cerebrally
inspired programme: it is a programme

that can be implemented with fair success at the lower levels of lifelessness, though even there incompletely, but which always represents a defective ideal of explanation and one less and less successful at the level of the living and the conscious. And it is our state of cerebral immersion which pushes most of the preparation for consciousness into the realm of the only dispositionally conscious, and so leads us to attribute to the cerebrum what only motivates its changes. On the whole it is arguable that, if we live in a cave, seeing only broken and puzzling reflections of being, that cave is the cerebrum, or, varying the metaphor, that the cerebrum is the high prison, enclosed by the skull-bones, where we see and deal with all in a perhaps biologically advantageous but philosophically confused manner. Still as philosophy thrives on confusion we may perhaps bless the cerebrum for making philosophy possible.

To what do these reflections finally tend? To the suggestion that there may be forms of conscious being-in-the-world, in

which the behavioural and the phenomenological dimensions do not require mediation by all those infinitely elaborate
mechanisms found in the cerebrum and
characteristic of 'our present state.' They
will be forms of conscious being in which
we shall not have to strike a compromise
with the scrofulous tenantry who now
make up our bodies and shall not have to
do everything through their restrictive,
often recalcitrant instrumentality. Bodies
we shall have, no doubt, having some of
the features of our present bodies, and in
them and through them we shall show
ourselves to other beings similarly embod-
ied, and act and be acted on by them and
by an environment which will serve as a
common background to us all, but these
bodies and their common environment will
have some traits of the imaginary as well
as the compulsively real, always mixing
the objectively invariant with the sub-
jectively modifiable. But as we progress
up the scale, corporeality will be attenuated to a mere reminiscence, to the
*commensurationes* with body which, ac-

cording to Thomas, attend upon and lend individuality to, even the most disembodied spirituality. Our present dim but strong sense of the interior life of others, hidden and revealed by their outer actions, will perhaps yield to a temporary incorporation of their experiences among our own to be succeeded by as prompt a fission and separation. Thomas's account of the social life of the 'separated substances' has much light to throw on these interesting possibilities. And instances and their hardness and sheer multiplicity will vanish, or will at most be vanishing illustrations and images of those substantial universals which are the true goal of our inductive exercises, and which will no doubt be seen to culminate in a truly substantial and central Universal of Universals, wholly unexhausted by the endless forms in which it is specified or instantiated, the centre of being hinted at by Plato and Plotinus, and with more confusion by Aristotle, and not very different from the God set forth in the persuasive paradoxes of Thomas.

At any rate I would suggest that this

world and its phenomena are only the
outer perimeter of a total world, incapable
of being understood unless we take account of an inner dimension in which it
narrows towards unity, and which we as
conscious beings are able to run up and
down, from the hardness of sense-percep-
tion up to the deepest states of self-collec-
tion and concentration and down again,
neither limit of which makes sense without
the other and without the whole interven-
ing spectrum. If you wish to consider my
speculative suggestions on these points,
you may read the later chapters of my
*Transcendence of the Cave*. But in the
light of all this total geography the problems of the cerebrum will be seen to be
those of a point on two intersecting lines,
one which places it in the perimeter of
things, hardly exclusive of and outwardly
connected with other things on the same
perimeter, while the other makes it the
outer extremity of a line leading up to the
centre of the world, in whose unitive sense
"all things come together." It is because
of this equivocal position that the cere-

brum is so tantalizing an object to meditate upon, and I cannot hope that my talk on this occasion will have done more than show why it is so utterly tantalizing.

I may in conclusion remark that I am very glad to have been asked to give the annual Aquinas Lecture at Marquette. Thomas in my view was an inconceivably original thinker who, while giving the appearance of being a humble interpreter and justifier of the views of "the philosopher" and the dogmas of the Christian faith, really transformed both profoundly, so that what he taught holds illumination even for those who are inclined to question Aristotle and who are perhaps not Catholics or Christians at all. Thomas made use of Aristotelian, and to an even greater, if covert, extent of Platonic conceptions (derived in a left-handed manner from a Syrian monk who had studied Proclus) to frame a notion of Deity which, while preserving the religious preeminence given to God by the Jews, yet managed to give this notion a viable and intelligible, and not merely anthropomor-

phic and pictorial sense. He also used
Aristotelian notions of the Soul, and Platonic notions that hovered behind them,
to achieve a unique synthesis of the cor-
poreal and the incorporeal, preserving the
former in even his most rarefied utterances
about the latter and vice versa. To those
who still need such things as an Ontology,
a Theology or Absolute-theory, and such
things as a Rational Psychology, Axiology
and Eschatology, Aquinas will remain a
necessary object of attention and study,
whether or not the Church which he orna-
mented continues to study and honour
him. If the worst comes to the worst, he
will have to be taken over by the *Gentiles*,
the heathen philosophers whom he so
manfully struggled to convert, much as
the Christian religion, extinct in Jerusa-
lem, had to be taken over and to find
stature and splendour in Alexandria, Con-
stantinople, Rome and other centres. The
worst will not, however, come to the worst,
and I remain deeply honoured by my as-
sociation, even if only through the title of
the present lecture, with the 'dumb ox' of

Aquino who, together with Plato, Plotinus, Hegel and a few others, is among my most valued intellectual mentors and solaces.

J. N. FINDLAY
Clark Professor of Moral
Philosophy and
Metaphysics
Yale University.

# The Aquinas Lectures

Published by the Marquette University Press
Milwaukee, Wisconsin 53233

❧

*St. Thomas and the Life of Learning* (1937) by
John F. McCormick, S.J., (1874-1943) professor of philosophy, Loyola University.

sbn 87462-101-1

*St. Thomas and the Gentiles* (1938) by Morti-
mer J. Adler, Ph.D., director of the Institute of
Philosophical Research, San Francisco, Calif.

sbn 87462-102-X

*St. Thomas and the Greeks* (1939) by Anton C.
Pegis, Ph.D., professor of philosophy, Pontifical Institute of Mediaeval Studies, Toronto.

sbn 87462-103-8

*The Nature and Functions of Authority* (1940)
by Yves Simon, Ph.D., (1903-1961) professor
of philosophy of social thought, University of
Chicago. sbn 87462-104-6

*St. Thomas and Analogy* (1941) by Gerald B.
Phelan, Ph.D., (1892-1965) professor of philosophy, St. Michael's College, Toronto.

sbn 87462-105-4

*St. Thomas and the Problem of Evil* (1942) by
Jacques Maritain, Ph.D., professor *emeritus*
of philosophy, Princeton University.

sbn 87462-106-2

*Humanism and Theology* (1943) by Werner
Jaeger, Ph.D., Litt.D., (1888-1961) University
professor, Harvard University. sbn 87462-107-0

*The Nature and Origins of Scientism* (1944) by John Wellmuth. <small>sbn 87462-108-9</small>

*Cicero in the Courtroom of St. Thomas Aquinas* (1945) by E. K. Rand, Ph.D., Litt.D., LL.D., (1871-1945) Pope professor of Latin, *emeritus,* Harvard University. <small>sbn 87462-109-7</small>

*St. Thomas and Epistemology* (1946) by Louis-Marie Regis, O.P., Th.L., Ph.D., director of the Albert the Great Institute of Mediaeval Studies, University of Montreal.
<small>sbn 87462-110-0</small>

*St. Thomas and the Greek Moralists* (1947, Spring) by Vernon J. Bourke, Ph.D., professor of philosophy, St. Louis University, St. Louis, Missouri. <small>sbn 87462-111-9</small>

*History of Philosophy and Philosophical Education* (1947, Fall) by Étienne Gilson of the *Académie française,* director of studies and professor of the history of Mediaeval philosophy, Pontifical Institute of Mediaeval Studies, Toronto. <small>sbn 87462-112-7</small>

*The Natural Desire for God* (1948) by William R. O'Connor, S.T.L., Ph.D., former professor of dogmatic theology, St. Joseph's Seminary, Dunwoodie, N.Y. <small>sbn 87462-113-5</small>

*St. Thomas and the World State* (1949) by Robert M. Hutchins, former Chancellor of the University of Chicago, president of the Fund for the Republic. <small>sbn 87462-114-3</small>

*Method in Metaphysics* (1950) by Robert J. Henle, S.J., Ph.D., academic vice-president, St. Louis University, St. Louis, Missouri.
sbn 87462-115-1

*Wisdom and Love in St. Thomas Aquinas* (1951) by Étienne Gilson of the *Académie française*, director of studies and professor of the history of Mediaeval philosophy, Pontifical Institute of Mediaeval Studies, Toronto.
sbn 87462-116-X

*The Good in Existential Metaphysics* (1952) by Elizabeth G. Salmon, Ph.D., professor of philosophy in the graduate school, Fordham University.
sbn 87462-117-8

*St. Thomas and the Object of Geometry* (1953) by Vincent Edward Smith, Ph.D., director, Philosophy of Science Institute, St. John's University.
sbn 87462-118-6

*Realism and Nominalism Revisited* (1954) by Henry Veatch, Ph.D., professor and chairman of the department of philosophy, Northwestern University.
sbn 87462-119-4

*Imprudence in St. Thomas Aquinas* (1955) by Charles J. O'Neil, Ph.D., professor of philosophy, Villanova University.
sbn 87462-120-8

*The Truth That Frees* (1956) by Gerard Smith, S.J., Ph.D., professor of philosophy, Marquette University.
sbn 87462-121-6

*St. Thomas and the Future of Metaphysics* (1957) by Joseph Owens, C.Ss.R., Ph.D., professor of philosophy, Pontifical Institute of Mediaeval Studies, Toronto.  SBN 87462-122-4

*Thomas and the Physics of 1958: A Confrontation* (1958) by Henry Margenau, Ph.D., Eugene Higgins professor of physics and natural philosophy, Yale University.
SBN 87462-123-2

*Metaphysics and Ideology* (1959) by Wm. Oliver Martin, Ph.D., professor of philosophy, University of Rhode Island.  SBN 87462-124-0

*Language, Truth and Poetry* (1960) by Victor M. Hamm, Ph.D., professor of English, Marquette University.  SBN 87462-125-9

*Metaphysics and Historicity* (1961) by Emil L. Fackenheim, Ph.D., professor of philosophy, University of Toronto.  SBN 87462-126-7

*The Lure of Wisdom* (1962) by James D. Collins, Ph.D., professor of philosophy, St. Louis University.  SBN 87462-127-5

*Religion and Art* (1963) by Paul Weiss, Ph.D. Sterling professor of philosophy, Yale University.  SBN 87462-128-3

*St. Thomas and Philosophy* (1964) by Anton C. Pegis, Ph.D., professor of philosophy, Pontifical Institute of Mediaeval Studies, Toronto.
SBN 87462-129-1

*The University In Process* (1965) by John O. Riedl, Ph.D., dean of faculty, Queensboro Community College.   sbn 87462-130-5

*The Pragmatic Meaning of God* (1966) by Robert O. Johann, associate professor of philosophy, Fordham University.

sbn 87462-131-3

*Religion and Empiricism* (1967) by John E. Smith, Ph.D., professor of philosophy, Yale University.   sbn 87462-132-1

*The Subject* (1968) by Bernard Lonergan, S.J., S.T.D., professor of Dogmatic Theology, Regis College, Ontario and Gregorian University, Rome.   sbn 87462-133-X

*Beyond Trinity* (1969) by Bernard J. Cooke, S.T.D.   sbn 87462-134-8

*Ideas and Concepts* (1970) by Julius R. Weinberg, Ph.D., (1908-1971) Vilas Professor of Philosophy, University of Wisconsin.

sbn 87462-135-6

*Reason and Faith Revisited* (1971) by Francis H. Parker, Ph.D., head of the philosophy department, Purdue University, Lafayette, Indiana.   sbn 87462-136-4

*Psyche and Cerebrum* (1972) by John N. Findlay, M.A. Oxon., Ph.D., Clark Professor of Moral Philosophy and Metaphysics, Yale University.   isbn 0-87462-137-2

Uniform format, cover and binding.